People
Everywhere

Acknowledgments

Executive Editor: Diane Sharpe
Supervising Editor: Stephanie Muller
Design Manager: Sharon Golden
Page Design: Simon Balley Design Associates
Photography: Biofotos: page 24; Greg Evans: page 12; The Hutchinson Library: pages 8, 10, 18, 20; Christine Osborne: page 16; Tony Stone Worldwide: page 6; Viewfinder: page 14; Wayland Picture Library: page 22: Zefa: page 26.

Library of Congress Cataloging-in-Publication Data

Humphrey, Paul, 1952-
     People everywhere/Paul Humphrey; illustrated by Colin King.
         p.   cm. — (Read all about it)
     Includes index.
     ISBN 0-8114-5728-1 Hardcover
     ISBN 0-8114-3722-1 Softcover
     1. Indigenous peoples — Juvenile literature.   2. Culture — Juvenile literature.   3. Life style — Juvenile literature. [1. Indigenous peoples. 2. Culture.] I. King, Colin, ill. II. Title. III. Series: Read all about it (Austin, Tex.)
GN380.H86   1995
904—dc20

94-28426
CIP
AC

People
Everywhere

Paul Humphrey

Illustrated by

Colin King

STECK-VAUGHN
COMPANY
ELEMENTARY • SECONDARY • ADULT • LIBRARY

There are people all over
the world. Climb aboard
the magic carpet so we can
meet some of them.

4

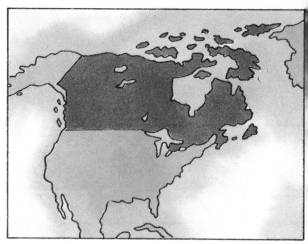

This Inuit girl
lives near the
North Pole in Canada.

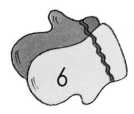

6

She is wearing very warm clothes.

7

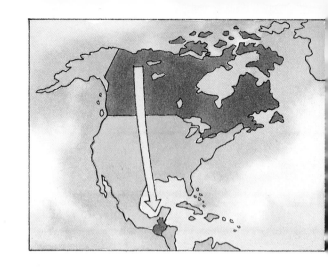

This girl is a
weaver from
Guatemala in Central America.
She makes shawls and blankets.

8

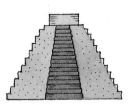

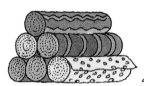

This boy is
from the
Amazon rain forest in Brazil.
He is feeding some macaws.

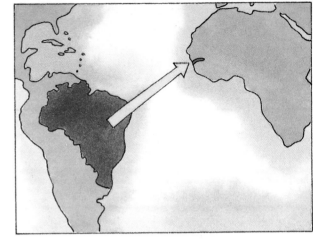

This woman
is from
Gambia in Africa. She is carrying
a bowl on her head.

12

13

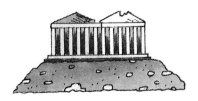

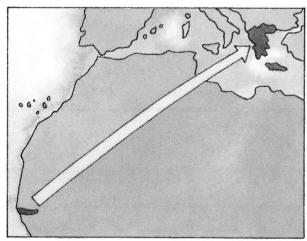

This girl is
from Greece.
She is leading her donkey.

14

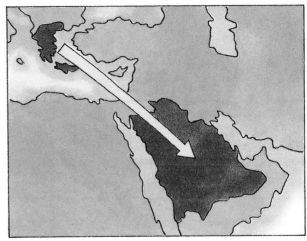

This man is
from the
desert land of Saudi Arabia.
He wears loose, white clothes.

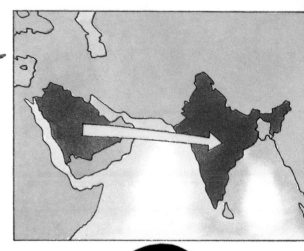

This woman
lives in India.
She is baking
Indian bread for
her supper.

19

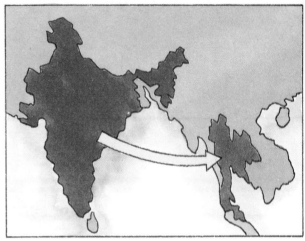

This family
lives in a
stilt house in Thailand. The stilts
keep the house from flooding when
it rains.

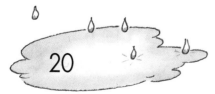

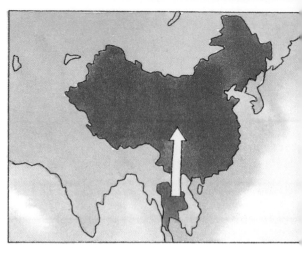

This man is a storyteller from China. I wonder what story he is telling.

22

My mom tells great stories.

23

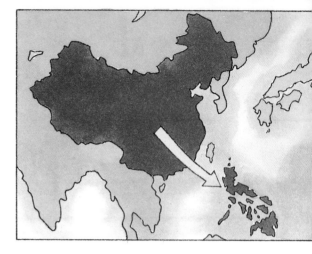

These people
are from the
Philippines. Look at their
beautiful fishing boat.

25

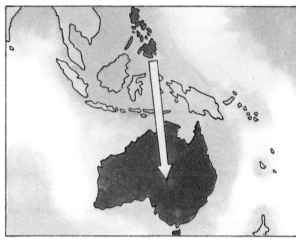

This man is
from Australia.
He is shearing a sheep.

My sweater is made from sheep's wool.

27

People around the world are very different. But we are all the same, too.

We all have to eat and drink.

We all need a place to live.

28

Now it's time
to go home.

29

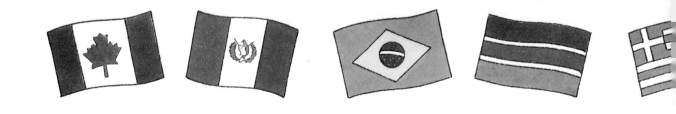

Look at the map. Do you remember the names of the places we visited?

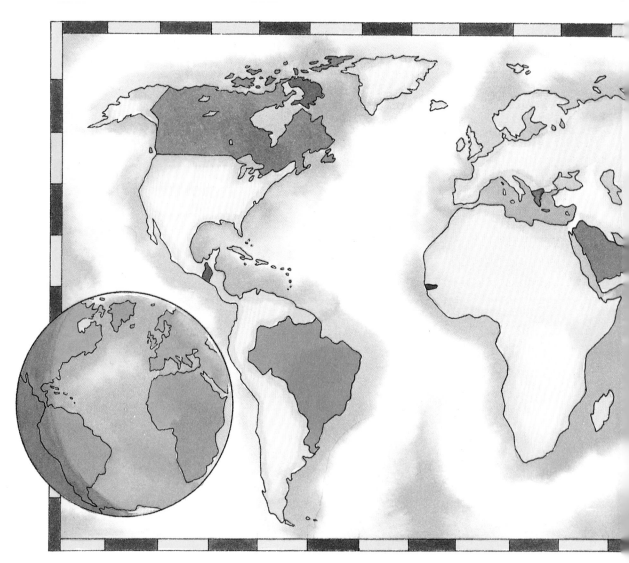

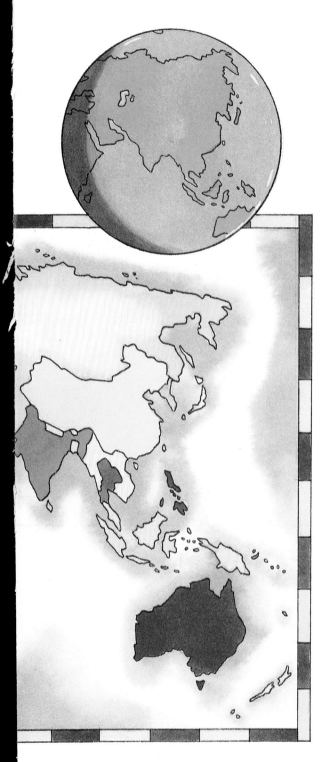

Index